AF400820

DARBY, LOVE...

DARBY, LOVE...

(ALIVE THINGS
MOM SAID TO ME
BEFORE SHE DIED)

Darby Hudson

Andrews McMeel
PUBLISHING®

The authorised representative in the EEA is Simon and Schuster
Netherlands BV, Herculesplein 96 3584 AA Utrecht, Netherlands.
(info@simonandschuster.nl)

Andrews McMeel Publishing
a division of Andrews McMeel Universal
1130 Walnut Street, Kansas City, Missouri 64106
www.andrewsmcmeel.com

26 27 28 29 30 VEP 10 9 8 7 6 5 4 3

ISBN: 979-8-8816-0725-8

Library of Congress Control Number: 2025940120

Editor: Kate Zimmermann
Art Director: Diane Marsh
Production Editor: Kelsey Rolofson
Production Manager: Chadd Keim

ATTENTION: SCHOOLS AND BUSINESSES
Andrews McMeel books are available at quantity discounts with
bulk purchase for educational, business, or sales promotional use.
For information, please email the Andrews McMeel Publishing
Special Sales Department: sales@andrewsmcmeel.com.

"Darby, love, have you ever noticed how the
dedication in a book is the most honest,
true, and lovely thing the author will
write before they start trying? Imagine
a book where all the pages are just
dedications. That would be a magical book."

INTRODUCTION

Mom was a stranger to this world. She belonged to one of magic and dreams. On her good days, she was unstoppable—pure spirit. And while her darkness was pure despair, it was countered, almost out of necessity, with the most incredible light. Mom's magic was the quiet eye of her confetti tornado.

And in these current times—in a world that can feel so dark—I want to share Mom's brightest self.

These pages hold the truth of most of what Mom did and said, but they're also an inspired love letter to her voice, capturing and channeling the spirit of the strangest, most poetic soul I've ever known.

Some of the most "famous" people I've ever met have no followers, no audience. Mom was one of those people. I was lucky to call her Mom, even if her lingering spirit still drives me up the wall sometimes.

Darby

(ALIVE THINGS MOM SAID TO ME BEFORE SHE DIED)

"DARBY, LOVE, LET'S WATCH OURSELVES ON THE
SUPERMARKET CCTV FOR A FEW MINUTES BEFORE
I BUY MY SMOKES. AREN'T WE JUST MAGICAL?!"

"DARBY, LOVE, IT WAS FOUR IN THE MORNING, SO I WENT FOR A WANDER IN THE STREETS IN MY BATHROBE AND LOCKED MYSELF OUT. BUT THEN I MET TWO LOVELY, DRUNK YOUNG MEN WHO DANCED WITH ME ON THE STREET UNTIL DAYLIGHT, AND EVENTUALLY A NEIGHBOR WITH A SPARE KEY WOKE UP AND LET ME IN."

3

"DARBY, LOVE, IT WAS A BEAUTIFUL
DAY, AND A LADYBUG TRAVELED ON MY
PERSON FOR MILES AND MILES."

I CALL MOM

MOM MAKES PIGEON COOING SOUNDS

I WHISTLE BIRD SOUNDS BACK

WE LAUGH

CALL ENDS

"DARBY, LOVE, AN ADULT WILL PLACE A FLOWER
NEXT TO A DYING BEE TO COMMEMORATE IT.
BUT A CHILD WILL PLACE A FLOWER NEXT TO
A DYING BEE TO GIVE IT THE WILL TO LIVE."

"DARBY, LOVE, ALWAYS HAVE A BUNCH OF
FLOWERS DELIVERED TO THE PLACES WHERE
UNEXPECTED HAPPINESS MOVED THROUGH YOU."

(ALIVE THINGS MOM SAID TO ME BEFORE SHE DIED)

"DARBY, LOVE, WHEN YOU GO FOR A WALK,
REMEMBER TO TELL THINGS YOU LOVE THEM
ALOUD. TREES, CLOUDS, FIRE HYDRANTS.
TELL ALL THE THINGS YOU LOVE THEM."

"DARBY, LOVE, IT'S HARD TO NOTICE WHAT ISN'T THERE: BIRDLESS TREES, TREELESS WINDS. TAKE THE TIME TO NOTICE WHAT'S MISSING, LOVE. ALSO, DO YOU KNOW WHERE I PUT MY CIGARETTES?"

"DARBY, LOVE, I BOUGHT THIS DOG
LEASH TODAY, AND I THINK IT WILL
MAKE THE PERFECT CLOTHESLINE."

"DARBY, LOVE, I BOUGHT A KITE TODAY TO
SAIL ON THE BEACH. LET'S GO FLY IT."

"DARBY, LOVE, THE MORNING SKY IS FRESHLY DOG-BARKED. LET'S GO OUT AND GET UNDER IT."

"DARBY, LOVE, IF YOU THINK ABOUT IT,
WALKING A DOG ON A VERY LONG LEASH IS
REALLY JUST FLYING A GROUND-KITE."

"DARBY, LOVE, LOOK AT THIS LITTLE SPECK OF SAND; I CAN SEE SO MUCH IN IT. THE WILD COLORS. EVERYTHING. ISN'T IT SOMETHING?!"

"DARBY, LOVE, TREES MOVE SO SLOWLY, AND
BIRDS ARE FAST AND TWITCHY, YET THEY
COHABITATE. THE UNIVERSE BALANCING
ITSELF OUT BEFORE OUR VERY EYES!"

"DARBY, LOVE, UNTIL I SEE SOMETHING, IT DOESN'T EXIST. HOW DO I KNOW MY BEDROOM EXISTS RIGHT NOW UNLESS I ENTER IT? ANYWAY, I BETTER START CRACKING ON THIS BRIEF FOR A CLIENT; AFTER ALL, I'M SUPPOSEDLY AN ATTORNEY. MAYBE MY CLIENT DOESN'T EXIST."

"DARBY, LOVE, WHY BOTHER BUYING A
HUGE TV? I JUST SIT INCHES AWAY
FROM THE SMALL ONE ON MY DESK."

"DARBY, LOVE, I'VE DECORATED MY PLACE
WITH OFFICE SUPPLIES. CHECK OUT ALL THE
CRISP DOCUMENTS ON MY BEAUTIFUL DESK!"

"DARBY, LOVE, I'VE BEEN WATCHING
DOCUMENTARIES OF THE UNIVERSE AND TAKING
PHOTOS OF THE TV AS I TRAVEL THROUGH
THE OUTER STRETCHES OF THE COSMOS . . .
WOWEE, LOVE, YOU'RE REALLY MISSING OUT!"

"DARBY, LOVE, GOD FORBID—DON'T EVER
DO HARD DRUGS; THEY WILL DESTROY
YOUR MIND. I NEVER HAVE. AND ON A
COMPLETELY UNRELATED TOPIC, I'VE SEEN
PEOPLE LEVITATE WITH MY OWN EYES."

"DARBY, LOVE, NEVER APOLOGIZE FOR SOMETHING,
THEN FART. IT'S NOT A TIME TO RELAX."

"DARBY, LOVE, I'M FULL OF SECRETS. WOULD YOU LIKE TO KNOW ONE? WELL, I'M NOT TELLING."

"DARBY, LOVE, IT'S NICE TO GO FOR A WALK AROUND THE BLOCK AT NIGHT THROUGH THE DARKNESS TO COME HOME TO THE SMALL, WARM LIGHT THROUGH YOUR FRONT WINDOW. BRIGHT AS A LIGHTHOUSE WRAPPED IN A STORM! WHY DO I FEEL MORE AT HOME IN THIS WORLD WHEN I'M ON THE OUTSIDE LOOKING IN?"

"DARBY, LOVE, WHENEVER YOU SEE A DEAD
KANGAROO BY THE SIDE OF THE ROAD,
ALWAYS CHECK IT BECAUSE THERE MIGHT BE
JOEYS IN THE POUCH THAT ARE ALIVE."

"DARBY, LOVE, I REMEMBER MY DREAM
FROM THE PREVIOUS NIGHT WHEN I LAY
MY HEAD ON THE PILLOW, SO DREAMS
MUST BE STORED IN PILLOWS!"

"DARBY, LOVE, I CAN HAVE A DREAM ABOUT
HAVING A MILLION DOLLARS, BUT WHEN I WAKE
UP, IT DOESN'T EXIST. BUT I CAN HAVE A DREAM
ABOUT A SONG THAT I'VE NEVER HEARD, AND
WHEN I WAKE UP, I CAN HUM IT! NUMBERS DON'T
WORK IN DREAMS, BUT MUSIC DOES. AND THAT'S
ALL I NEED TO KNOW ABOUT EVERYTHING."

"DARBY, LOVE, I WAS IN A BAD MOOD, SO I WENT FOR A WALK, BUT THE SUN WAS SO BRIGHT, I SCRUNCHED MY FACE. IT MUST HAVE LOOKED LIKE A SMILE, BECAUSE EVERYONE WAS SMILING BACK AT ME, SO I FELT A LOT BETTER."

"DARBY, LOVE, LIFE ISN'T NAILED TOGETHER
WITH NUMBERS AND FACTS. IT'S FLIMSILY HELD
TOGETHER WITH BIRDSONG, FADING SUNSETS,
AND STRAY CATS UNDER PARKED CARS."

"DARBY, LOVE, EVEN THAT PIECE OF LITTER
IS A CLUE TO THE POEM OF SOMEONE
ELSE'S WHOLE LIFE, THE TIP OF AN
ICEBERG TO SOMEONE'S WHOLE WORLD.
WE ARE DETECTIVES OF INCREDIBLE,
ENDLESS MYSTERIES. AND POETS ARE LIKE
DETECTIVES, EXCEPT DETECTIVES SOLVE
MYSTERIES, AND POETS DEEPEN MYSTERIES."

(ALIVE THINGS MOM SAID TO ME BEFORE SHE DIED)

"DARBY, LOVE, SOMETIMES I WONDER IF I'VE
FELT ALL THE EMOTIONS AVAILABLE IN THIS
LIFE. I'M THANKFUL THAT SLEEPING DREAMS
BORROW AND MIX ALL THE THINGS WE FEEL
IN WAKING REALITY TO CREATE BRAND-NEW
EMOTIONS. THAT'S WHY I'VE JUST WOKEN UP
AND AM DEEPLY BUT PLEASANTLY CONFUSED."

"DARBY, LOVE, YES, MY PLACE IS MESSY, BUT I'VE TURNED MY KITCHEN TRASH CAN INTO A FILING SYSTEM: GENERAL TRASH ON THAT SIDE, AND MORE IMPORTANT THINGS ON THIS SIDE OF THE CAN."

"DARBY, LOVE, I'VE HIGHLIGHTED ALL THE WORDS IN MY ENTIRE BOOK BECAUSE EVERYTHING IS IMPORTANT. AND I'VE PLACED A DIFFERENT-COLORED POST-IT NOTE ON EVERY PAGE OF NEARLY ALL MY BOOKS. AND NOW WHEN I FAN MY BOOKS, THEY LOOK LIKE PEACOCKS. HOW BEAUTIFUL."

"DARBY, LOVE, BOOKS ARE MADE OF TREES. AND YOU CAN READ TREES. YOU START AT THE TOP OF THE TREE, SCAN FROM LEFT TO RIGHT, AND REPEAT SLOWLY DOWNWARD. SOMETIMES A BIRD, SOMETIMES A FALLING LEAF, SOMETIMES A MOON THROUGH THE BRANCHES. IT'S A WHOLE STORY."

"DARBY, LOVE, I WANT THE SONG 'GLORIA'
BY LAURA BRANIGAN PLAYED AT MY
WEDDING—I MEAN FUNERAL."

"DARBY, LOVE, REMEMBER THAT DREAM YOU HAD ABOUT A MAGICAL CROW THAT LIVED INSIDE YOU AND SANG YOU SECRETS? NEVER TELL ANYONE ABOUT IT. IT'S AN IMPORTANT DREAM."

"DARBY, LOVE, I HAVE TO RUN NAKED
BETWEEN THE SHOWER AND MY BEDROOM
WITH 'FLIGHT OF THE BUMBLEBEE' TURNED
UP SO HIGH, THE WALLS VIBRATE BEFORE
I GET READY TO GO SOMEWHERE."

"DARBY, LOVE, I CAN'T TALK RIGHT NOW; I'M
LATE FOR AN APPOINTMENT. I'VE ALWAYS LIVED
IN MY OWN TIME ZONE. AND NO, THEY'RE NOT
EXPECTING ME. IT'S A SURPRISE APPOINTMENT."

"DARBY, LOVE, HAVE YOU HEARD OF ADAM ELLIOT? HIS NEW SHORT FILM, *HARVIE KRUMPET*, IS A WONDER! AND HE IS FROM MELBOURNE, TOO. THERE MUST BE SOMETHING IN THE WATER AND COFFEE HERE, LOVE."

"DARBY, LOVE, THE WORLD IS SO VAST,
INCREDIBLE, AND FULL OF WONDER;
THAT'S WHY I'M CRYING. AND BECAUSE
I DIDN'T PAY MY BILLS ON TIME."

"DARBY, LOVE, I GET HORIZONTIGO
LOOKING OUT ACROSS THE VANISHING
POINT OF THE OCEAN'S HORIZON, LIKE
I'M GOING TO FALL, BUT IN LOVE."

"DARBY, LOVE, THERE IS SO MUCH BEAUTY
IN THE WORLD. ALSO, I HOPE YOU'VE BEEN
KEEPING UP WITH THE POLITICS IN THIS
COUNTRY; TERRIBLE THINGS ARE HAPPENING.
OH, LOOK AT THAT CLOUD—IT LOOKS LIKE
A PELICAN! DO YOU SEE THAT, LOVE?!"

(ALIVE THINGS MOM SAID TO ME BEFORE SHE DIED)

"DARBY, LOVE, LET'S GO FOR A WALK
AND TALK TO EVERY STRANGER ON
THE STREET WHO SMILES AT US."

"DARBY, LOVE, IF SOMEONE ASKS HOW
YOU'RE DOING TODAY, LOOK OVER THEIR
SHOULDER, FOCUS ON THE FARTHEST POINT
OF THE HORIZON, AND IN A LOWERED
VOICE, ANSWER, 'INCREDIBLE.'"

"DARBY, LOVE, THERE'S NO SUCH THING AS
A COINCIDENCE; IT'S LIFE SHOWING YOU
THE WAY. SYMPHONIC SERENDIPITY."

"DARBY, LOVE, TREES ARE LIKE GIANT
PIANOS. THEY PLAY THEMSELVES IN THE
MORNINGS. THEN THERE'S AN INTERMISSION
OF HUMAN NOISE AND STUPIDITY. AND
THEN THEY PLAY AGAIN IN THE
EVENINGS. AND THEN IT'S BEDTIME."

"DARBY, LOVE, SO FOR WEEKS YOU WERE
TEXTING YOURSELF YOUR HOPES, DREAMS,
AND MAGICAL THOUGHTS BUT DISCOVERED
YOU HAD BEEN ACCIDENTALLY TEXTING
THEM TO A STRANGER THE WHOLE TIME? AND
EVENTUALLY THEY RESPONDED AND ASKED,
'WHO IS THIS?' AND THEN YOU ASKED THEM
TO BE YOUR HONORARY GUARDIAN ANGEL,
AND THEY RESPONDED WITH 'YES'? YOU'RE
ON THE RIGHT PATH, LOVE. KEEP GOING."

"DARBY, LOVE, THERE'S NO NEED TO SWEAR
IN YOUR POETRY. BUT I DO LIKE YOUR
HANDMADE CONFETTI WITH 'GET FUCKED'
PRINTED ON EACH COLORFUL PIECE.
THAT'S FUNNY. BUT REALLY, LOVE?"

"DARBY, LOVE, NEARLY ALL HUMAN MEASURING
TOOLS FOR WHAT IS VALUABLE AND TRUE IN
THIS LIFE ARE CORRUPT OR WRONG. AT SOME
POINT, YOU HAVE TO CREATE YOUR OWN SCALES
FOR WHAT IS REAL IN THIS WORLD. BORROW
FROM THE UNKNOWN. EVEN IF IT LOOKS
RIDICULOUS AND INSANE TO NEARLY EVERYONE."

"DARBY, LOVE, EVERYTHING IS RIDICULOUS
AND EVERYONE IS SERIOUS."

"DARBY, LOVE, THERE'S SO MUCH SADNESS
IN THE WORLD, YET I'M ALWAYS FALLING
IN LOVE WITH THE DAY. THERE'S ALMOST
TOO MUCH TO FALL IN LOVE WITH."

"DARBY, LOVE, I'VE BEEN READING THE OBITUARIES IN THE NEWSPAPER EVERY DAY. YOU GET TO MY AGE AND THAT'S WHAT YOU DO. WHAT A RELIEF TO HAVE THE WEIGHT OF A LIFE REDUCED TO ONE SENTENCE."

(ALIVE THINGS MOM SAID TO ME BEFORE SHE DIED)

"DARBY, LOVE, SOMEWHERE DEEP DOWN, AGAINST
ALL EVIDENCE, NO ONE THINKS THEY'RE
ACTUALLY GOING TO DIE. THAT ONLY HAPPENS
TO OTHER PEOPLE. BUT IN THE STRANGEST WAY,
IT'S KIND OF TRUE—WE NEVER TRULY DIE."

"DARBY, LOVE, I'M LATE BECAUSE I LOST MY
CAR KEYS. BUT I WASN'T EVEN FRUSTRATED.
IN FACT, I WAS THRILLED! FOR A MOMENT,
THERE WAS NO LOGICAL EXPLANATION. IT
WAS THE DIVINE MYSTERY OF THE MISSING
CAR KEYS, AND THE WORLD IS LACKING IN
SMALL MYSTERIES. BUT THEN I FOUND THEM
IN MY CAR DOOR, AND IT WAS SADLY BACK
TO REALITY AND TURNING UP LATE."

"DARBY, LOVE, LIFE IS A WALK IN THE PARK,
BUT WITH RABID STRAY DOGS AND SOMEONE
LOOKING TO MUG YOU. BUT ON A BEAUTIFUL DAY,
OF COURSE. AND THAT'S ALL THAT MATTERS."

"DARBY, LOVE, SOMETIMES I GET THE FEELING THAT THERE'S SOMETHING VERY WRONG WITH ME, AND THEN ANOTHER FEELING COMES RUSHING IN FROM BEHIND SAYING THERE'S SOMETHING VERY RIGHT WITH ME."

"DARBY, LOVE, DON'T EVER PUT ANYTHING
IN WRITING EXCEPT FOR POETRY. NO
ONE CAN ACCUSE YOU OF POETRY."

"DARBY, LOVE, LET'S GO OPEN MY OVERDUE BILL
ON THE BEACH WHILE WATCHING AN INCREDIBLE
SUNSET AND SEE WHICH EMOTION WINS."

"DARBY, LOVE, YOUR SPECIAL CEMETERY GARDEN
IS BEAUTIFUL. THERE'S SO MUCH LIFE HERE—
PEPPERCORN TREES, CROWS SINGING, LITTLE
INSECTS CATCHING THE SUN. THANK YOU FOR
TAKING ME HERE. ISN'T IT INTERESTING
HOW THE CITY BUILDINGS IN THE DISTANCE
LOOK LIKE A PARKING LOT OF SILENT GIANT
GRAVESTONES RISING OUT OF THE GROUND?"

"DARBY, LOVE, AT WHAT POINT DOES
SCIENCE SEPARATE THE WIND FROM THE
TREE? LET'S STILL BELIEVE A TREE
CHURNS AND MOVES BY ITSELF."

"DARBY, LOVE, SOMETIMES I LIKE TO GO FOR A WANDER IN PUBLIC DURING THE DAY IN MY BATHROBE AND I FEEL LIKE ONE OF THOSE BOXERS ENTERING THE RING. SOME PEOPLE THINK I'M LOST AND OFFER ME MONEY. I TELL THEM, 'NO, I'M JUST OFF TO FEED THE BIRDS,' THEN WINK AND SMILE AT THEM."

"DARBY, LOVE, AM I NORMAL? MAYBE
NOT. BUT WHAT IS NORMAL?"

"DARBY, LOVE, MY OLD, BARELY WORKING
RECORD PLAYER WOBBLES OUT MUSIC LIKE
IT'S HAUNTED. I CAN'T AFFORD TO FIX IT, BUT
I'VE COME TO LIKE HAUNTED TCHAIKOVSKY
AND HANDEL. IT'S STILL INCREDIBLE."

"DARBY, LOVE, HERE'S YOUR BIRTHDAY PRESENT:
A THREE-PACK OF TOOTHBRUSHES, A BEAUTIFUL
FEATHER, AND AN INTERESTING-LOOKING
PEBBLE I FOUND. USEFUL AND MAGICAL THINGS."

"DARBY, LOVE, THIS VIDEO GAME, *DOUBLE DRAGON*, THAT YOU PLAYED ON AN ARCADE MACHINE AT THE DELI . . . DID YOU SAY THERE ARE LADIES IN THE GAME WEARING LYCRA AND WIELDING WHIPS? THAT'S HORRENDOUS! TAKE ME TO SEE IT. I'M FASCINATED."

"DARBY, LOVE, SOMETIMES I THINK I'M
JUST TOO ALIVE. IS THERE SUCH A
THING AS BEING TOO ALIVE?"

"DARBY, LOVE, YOU'RE NEVER ALONE. AND WE'RE ALSO TERRIBLY ALONE. BOTH AT ONCE. THE WIND, THE STARS, AND THE BIRDS ARE ALL BEAUTIFUL STRANGERS."

"DARBY, LOVE, I WAS OUT FOR A WALK, AND
A SENIOR CITIZEN—OLDER THAN I AM—
ASKED ME WHAT DAY IT WAS, AND I SAID
'TUESDAY.' AND MOMENTS LATER, I REALIZED
IT WAS A MONDAY. SO AS SHE WALKED AWAY,
I CHUCKLED TO MYSELF, THINKING I'D
ACCIDENTALLY GIVEN US BOTH AN EXTRA DAY
TO LIVE. I-HAVE-NO-IDEA-WHAT-DAY-IT-IS IS
ALWAYS MY FAVORITE DAY OF THE WEEK."

"DARBY, LOVE, BECAUSE WE HAVE TONGUES,
WE'RE PRETTY MUCH IN CHARGE OF A
TENTACLE! AND SOMETIMES IT'S IN
THERE DOING ITS OWN THING!"

"DARBY, LOVE, I WEAR THIS BROKEN AND
TICK-LESS WATCH TO INTERVIEWS BECAUSE
IT TRICKS PEOPLE INTO THINKING I
KNOW WHAT I'M DOING, THAT I MIGHT
HAVE A PLAN, AND THAT I MIGHT HAVE TO
BE SOMEWHERE . . . AND VERY SOON."

"DARBY, LOVE, EVERYTHING YOU NEED
IS INSIDE OF YOU. HOW DO YOU LOOK
INSIDE OF YOU? YOU'LL KNOW WHEN
YOU NO LONGER HAVE A CHOICE."

"DARBY, LOVE, THE BILLS DON'T PAY
THEMSELVES. BUT THE POEMS WILL ALWAYS
WRITE THEMSELVES. I'M GLAD YOU PUT YOUR
OVERDUE BILL IN A LOVELY FRAME AND
SOLD IT AS ART FOR THE EXACT AMOUNT
DUE. WHEN POETRY PAYS THE BILLS, THAT IS
THE MAGIC: THE ART OF STAYING ALIVE."

"DARBY, LOVE, BECAUSE WE DIE AND JUST VANISH, TECHNICALLY ALL OUR FRIENDS ARE IMAGINARY FRIENDS. BUT THAT DOESN'T MEAN THEY'RE LESS REAL. IT MEANS WE'RE ALL MADE OF MAGIC."

"DARBY, LOVE, SOMETIMES I SECRETLY FEEL
SORRY FOR CLOUDS IN PHOTOS, IMPRISONED
IN THEM FOREVER, UNABLE TO CHANGE SHAPE
AGAIN. MAYBE THAT POO-SHAPED CLOUD
WANTED TO BLOSSOM INTO A FLOWER."

"DARBY, LOVE, I'M OLD AND ALL MY
FRIENDS ARE NOW DEAD. BUT MAYBE THE
FAIREST THING ABOUT LIFE IS DEATH."

"DARBY, LOVE, WHEN YOU'RE A CHILD, IT'S HARD TO TELL DREAMS FROM WAKING LIFE. THEN YOU GET OLDER—THE DREAM WORLD IS LOST, AND IT'S JUST BRUTAL REALITY: BILLS, BREAKDOWNS, AND BAD BLOOD. BUT AS I GET OLD, LIFE'S DREAMLIKE STRANGENESS IS RETURNING. THE BIRDS AND THE ANIMALS KNOW. IT'S BEAUTIFUL HERE, LOVE."

"DARBY, LOVE, I WAS STANDING IN THE EMPTY AISLE ALONE, A LITTLE LOST, JUST STARING THROUGH THE PRODUCTS ON THE SHELF. THEN THREE SEPARATE STRANGERS SUDDENLY APPEARED AND GATHERED NEXT TO ME FOR NO GOOD REASON. THEY THOUGHT I HAD FOUND WHAT THEY WERE LOOKING FOR! ISN'T THAT A FUNNY PHENOMENON, LOVE? THEY MUST HAVE THOUGHT I KNEW SOMETHING THAT THEY DIDN'T. BUT I WAS JUST MARVELOUSLY LOST IN THE MOMENT OF THE SUPERMARKET AISLE. I HOPE THEY ENJOYED IT AS MUCH AS I DID."

"DARBY, LOVE, SOMETIMES I'LL DIP INTO A
BOOK OF POETRY AND IT'S SO DREAMY, I'LL
LOOK UP FROM THE BOOK AND FEEL LIKE
I'VE CAUGHT A LINE TO ANOTHER WORLD."

"DARBY, LOVE, THAT PHOTO OF YOU BENDING OVER TO PAT A CHICKEN WHILE YOUR BOTTOM POINTS SKYWARD, THERE'S A COMPOSITIONAL GOLDEN RATIO TO IT—IT'S PERFECTLY RIDICULOUS. IT'S A VISUAL PERPETUAL MOTION MACHINE OF SILLINESS: MY EYES SWIRLING IN CIRCLES, ENDLESSLY CAUGHT BETWEEN YOUR SILLY BOTTOM AND THE SILLY CHICKEN."

"DARBY, LOVE, I'LL NEVER GET A MOBILE PHONE OR THE INTERNET CONNECTED. I KNOW I'M MISSING OUT, BUT I DON'T WANT ANYONE TO KNOW A THING ABOUT ME. I JUST NEED TO BE CONNECTED TO INSTANT COFFEE, CIGARETTES, AND MY WINDOW."

"DARBY, LOVE, I'M WRITING IN A DIFFERENT
DIARY EACH YEAR AND SPRAYING EACH
WITH A NEW PERFUME, SO WHEN I REREAD,
THE SCENT WILL TAKE ME BACK."

"DARBY, LOVE, YOU KNOW THAT FEELING WHEN YOU SEE A SUNSET, THE STARS, OR MOONLIGHT? PUT IT INTO EVERYTHING YOU DO. PUT A BIT OF MOONLIGHT INTO EVERYTHING. EVEN IF PEOPLE DON'T NOTICE, THEIR HEARTS WILL."

"DARBY, LOVE, YOU CAN FEEL THE INVISIBLE
TIDES OF THE MASSES—THE PUSH AND
PULL OF UNSEEN CROWDS. IT'S THE REASON
WHY THERE IS SUCH AN INCREDIBLE
PEACEFULNESS BETWEEN CHRISTMAS AND
NEW YEAR'S, BECAUSE EVERYONE IS DOING
NOTHING AT THE SAME TIME. WE ARE ANTENNAE
TO SOMETHING VAST AND INCREDIBLE."

"DARBY, LOVE, THANK YOU FOR TAKING ME TO YOUR SPECIAL SPOT BY THE TRAIN TRACKS. SORRY, LOVE, BUT I'M GOING TO SIT HERE UNDER THIS OLD TREE FOR THE REST OF THE NIGHT AND WATCH THE TRAINS GO BY WITH YOU. WATCHING COMMUTERS CATTLED PAST— THE TRAINS LIGHTING UP THIS RIVERBED OF STEEL LIKE INDUSTRIAL FIREWORKS— IS DREAMY. YOU CAN FEEL THE PATIENCE IN THE DIRT WHERE WE ARE SITTING AS THINGS HURRY PAST ON CONCRETE AND STEEL. A LIFE FROM THE SIDELINES."

(ALIVE THINGS MOM SAID TO ME BEFORE SHE DIED)

"DARBY, LOVE, NIGHT TREES SPEAK
TO ME IN A BRAILLE THAT STANDS
ON MY SHOULDERS AND ARMS!"

"DARBY, LOVE, SOME LONELINESSES CAN
NEVER BE SHARED. THEY'RE YOURS ALONE."

"DARBY, LOVE, I HAVEN'T TALKED TO ANYONE
IN THREE DAYS! I NEARLY FORGOT HOW TO
TALK! WHEN YOU'RE ALONE LONG ENOUGH,
YOU FORGET YOU'RE A PERSON. I STARTED
TO THINK I WAS THE TREE OUTSIDE MY
WINDOW, WATCHING AND MARVELING AT
ITSELF. IT'S RATHER NICE FEELING LEAFY."

"DARBY, LOVE, SOMETIMES I WAKE IN THE MORNING ON THE LIFE RAFT OF MY BED, WASHED TO SHORE WITHIN THE PARADISE OF A NEW DAY, AND EXIT THE SPACESHIP OF MY HOME INTO A NEW WORLD."

"DARBY, LOVE, THE FIRST TIME I STAYED UP
ALL NIGHT, IT FELT LIKE I'D DISCOVERED
A SECRET TUNNEL INTO TOMORROW. BUT
REALLY, WHEN I STAY UP ALL NIGHT, THE
REST OF THE WORLD GETS A DAY AHEAD
OF ME. AND I'VE BEEN DOING IT FOR
YEARS. MAYBE THAT'S WHY I LIKE READING
MY TWO-YEAR-OLD NEWSPAPERS?"

"DARBY, LOVE, I THINK I'M DYING.
BUT FIRST, LET'S GO PLAY."

"DARBY, LOVE, TELL ME YOUR
DREAMS. NOT YOUR AMBITIONS."

"DARBY, LOVE, I'VE NEVER FELT
TRULY AT HOME. EVERY PLACE I EVER
LIVED FELT LIKE CAMPING."

"DARBY, LOVE, NOT MUCH MAKES SENSE. BUT
WHY SHOULD IT? IT'S LIFE'S RESPONSIBILITY
TO REMAIN AS RIDICULOUS AS POSSIBLE
IN ALL ITS FUN AND SADNESS."

"DARBY, LOVE, I SAW A FIGURE DOWN THE STREET—A MILE AWAY—AND I COULD TELL IT WAS YOU SIMPLY FROM THE SHAPE OF YOUR WALK. THE WAY YOU WALK IS YOUR DNA IN MOTION; IT'S YOUR SPIRIT SADDLING YOUR BODY LIKE A HORSE AND TAKING IT FOR A RIDE. AND REMEMBER, LOVE, YOU'RE NEVER ALONE: ALL YOU HAVE TO DO IS SUMMON THE FAMILIARITY OF YOUR SPIRIT BY WALKING THE EARTH, EVEN IF IT'S DOWN TO THE SHOPS."

"DARBY, LOVE, MY MIND IS A MAZE I TRY TO
GET THROUGH: I ENTER IT IN THE MORNING
AND EXIT IT AT NIGHT. IT'S FULL OF TWISTS,
TURNS, AND MANY DEAD ENDS. THAT'S WHY I
LIKE STAYING UP ALL NIGHT—THERE'S NO
MAZE, JUST A LOVELY STRAIGHT BACK ROAD,
SO I HAVE TIME TO LOOK UP AT THE STARS."

"DARBY, LOVE, SOMETIMES TALKING TO MY
WALLS ALOUD HOLDS THE ANSWERS. I'VE ASKED
MY COMMITTEE OF WALLS QUESTIONS, AND
THEY USUALLY HAVE SOMETHING INTERESTING
TO SAY. BUT THE CEILING ALWAYS BRINGS
ME THE MOST HOPEFUL ANSWERS BECAUSE
I HAVE TO LOOK UP WHEN I TALK TO IT."

"DARBY, LOVE, AUTOMATIC DOOR SENSORS
WON'T RECOGNIZE ME WHEN I ENTER A SHOP,
AND THE SECURITY ALARM GOES OFF WHEN
I LEAVE THE SHOP. AND I HAVEN'T STOLEN
ANYTHING. WE ARE INVISIBLE AND GUILTY
IN THIS FAKE, HUMAN-MADE REALITY."

"DARBY, LOVE, THE FAINT SOUND OF 'HAPPY
BIRTHDAY' SUNG AT NIGHT FROM STREETS AWAY
MAKES ME SAD—IT SOUNDS LIKE MY CHILDHOOD
'HAPPY BIRTHDAY' SUNG FROM A LIFETIME AWAY."

(ALIVE THINGS MOM SAID TO ME BEFORE SHE DIED)

"DARBY, LOVE, EVERYONE IN THE STRIP MALL
KNOWS MY NAME. BUT I'VE FORGOTTEN THEIRS,
SO THEY MAKE ME PLAY NAME-GUESSING
GAMES. I JUST CAN'T REMEMBER ALL THEIR
NAMES. BUT NAMES DON'T REALLY MATTER, AND
WITHOUT THEM WE ARE IMMORTAL. I HAVE
THE MOST INTERESTING CONVERSATIONS WITH
PEOPLE WHEN I DON'T KNOW THEIR NAME.
EVERY PERSON IS AN INCREDIBLE WORLD IN
A VAST GALAXY. WHEN I TALK TO SOMEONE, I'M
ON THEIR PLANET, AND THEY'RE ON MINE."

"DARBY, LOVE, BELIEVE NOTHING YOU READ OR HEAR IN THE NEWS. AT BEST, THE NEWS IS A DISTRACTION OF LOW-QUALITY ENTERTAINMENT. THE SALES ADS IN THE NEWSPAPER ARE MORE GENUINE. DID YOU KNOW YOU CAN GET HALF-PRICE COMFY SOCKS RIGHT NOW?"

"DARBY, LOVE, STORIES NEED AN OBSTACLE—
SOMETHING TO OVERCOME. BUT AS A CHILD,
I DIDN'T NEED A STORY—ALL I NEEDED WAS
JUST A SCENE, A PICTURE, WHERE THERE
WAS NOTHING TO MAKE SENSE OF. MAYBE
SOMETHING AT NIGHT, IN THE RAIN, WITH
A LITTLE MOONLIGHT. A DREAM I COULD
ENTER INTO. I'M TIRED OF STORIES."

"DARBY, LOVE, ALL THE HATE IN THE WORLD IS SOLD TO YOU, AND ALL THE LOVE IN THE WORLD IS FREE."

"DARBY, LOVE, THE WORLD HATES MAGIC. IT'S THE REASON WHY THERE ARE NOW MORE ANSWERS IN THE WORLD THAN QUESTIONS. IT'S AS IF HUMANS TRADED CANDLELIT CAVE ART OF THE SOUL FOR 7-ELEVEN FLUORESCENT LIGHTS ILLUMINATING A RACK OF FASHION MAGAZINES."

"DARBY, LOVE, SOMETIMES I WONDER: HOW MANY SUNSETS IS A LIFE WORTH? EVEN JUST ONE WOULD BE ENOUGH. A SUNSET WITH A SIGH."

"DARBY, LOVE, I WAS IN THE PARK TODAY, AND I DIPPED MY HAND INTO THE REFLECTION OF MYSELF ON THE SURFACE OF A POND AND FELT A GOLDFISH BRUSH BETWEEN MY FINGERS—IT WAS AS IF I HAD TOUCHED A DREAM INSIDE OF MYSELF. I THOUGHT YOU SHOULD KNOW IN CASE I SAY ANYTHING A LITTLE ODD RIGHT NOW."

"DARBY, LOVE, I'VE KISSED THIS LITTLE
PEBBLE. NOW IT'S BLESSED. AND IT'S FOR YOU."

"DARBY, LOVE, LIFE OFTEN FEELS LIKE
ONE VERY LONG DAY WITH LOTS OF NAPS
AND BAD DECISIONS. AND A YEAR IS JUST A
BUNCH OF MONDAYS, THEN CHRISTMAS! BUT
SOMETIMES SIMPLY MAKING THE DAY TURN
UP IN ALL ITS MESS IS THE ONLY MAGIC
I'VE GOT LEFT. BUT IT'S MY MESS AND MAGIC.
AND I WOULDN'T WANT ANYONE ELSE'S."

"DARBY, LOVE, WATCH THE STARS—THEY'LL
RECHARGE THE TWINKLE IN YOUR EYE."

"DARBY, LOVE, SOMETIMES YOU'VE GOT TO GET THROUGH THE DAY AND INTO THE NIGHT USING YOUR SHADOW AS A SAIL."

"DARBY, LOVE, I KNOW MY CEILING IS
YELLOW FROM CIGARETTES, I KNOW I DRINK
TEN COFFEES A DAY, I KNOW MY LIFE IS
FALLING APART . . . BUT I HOPE YOU'RE
LOOKING AFTER YOURSELF, LOVE."

"DARBY, LOVE, NEVER FOOL AROUND WITH A OUIJA BOARD. IT'S NOT A TOY. IT'S VERY DANGEROUS. THERE ARE UNSEEN FORCES IN THIS WORLD THAT WOULD SURPRISE AND HORRIFY MOST PEOPLE. ASK THE *I CHING* A QUESTION INSTEAD. YOUR GUARDIAN ANGEL WILL ANSWER."

"DARBY, LOVE, I'VE BEEN AWAKE THREE
NIGHTS IN A ROW, SMOKING CIGARETTES
AND READING MYTHOLOGY, PHILOSOPHY, AND
THEOLOGY. READING IN THE MIDDLE OF THE
NIGHT WHEN EVERYONE IS ASLEEP IS MAGIC.
WHEN THE WHOLE WORLD IS SLEEPING, YOU
CAN ACTUALLY HEAR THE BOOK TALKING
TO YOU. DEAD AUTHORS ARE MORE ALIVE
THAN MOST PEOPLE WHO ARE LIVING."

"DARBY, LOVE, I KNOW ROUGHLY WHERE I AM. I'M RIGHT HERE, INSIDE MY LITTLE FLAT. BUT WE ARE ALL JUST A BUNCH OF MESSY FEELINGS CAUGHT SOMEWHERE BETWEEN THE DIRT AND THE STARS, ALIVE ON EARTH, FOR NOW."

"DARBY, LOVE, ONE DAY ALL THAT WILL
REMAIN OF YOU WILL BE THE ATMOSPHERE
OF A LINGERING SMILE YOU LEFT IN THE
STREET FROM A MOMENT OF UNEXPLAINED
HAPPINESS. A HAPPINESS THAT ARRIVED
WITHOUT A PLAN, A BEAUTIFUL GLITCH IN THE
SYSTEM. AND A LIFETIME FROM NOW, SOMEONE'S
GOING TO STROLL THROUGH THE SAME SPACE
WHERE YOU PLANTED THAT SMILE AND FEEL
GOOD FOR SEEMINGLY NO REASON AT ALL."

"DARBY, LOVE, ALL MY BOOKS HAVE A THICK
COAT OF DUST ON THEM. AT SOME POINT
THERE ARE ONLY SO MANY WORDS YOU CAN
READ UNTIL THEY'RE USELESS, AND FINALLY
ALL YOU NEED IS A WINDOW TO SOME SKY."

ME: MOM, DO YOU STILL LOVE THE WISDOM OF YODA FROM *STAR WARS*?

MOM: *SHAKES HER HEAD*

ME: DO YOU LIKE A DIFFERENT *STAR WARS* CHARACTER NOW?

MOM: YES. CHEWBACCA, BECAUSE HE CAN'T SPEAK HUMAN WORDS.

"DARBY, LOVE, I'M STRUGGLING TO FIT THIS ONE LIFE INTO THIS ONE LIFE. YET THERE ARE SO MANY LIVES I WISH I'D LIVED. BUT THEN I THINK, IN ALL THOSE LIVES, I'D STILL HAVE SEEN THE SAME MOON AT NIGHT."

"DARBY, LOVE, LOOK AT THAT SEAGULL FLYING
AND CIRCLING UP THERE, ABOVE ITS FLOCK
ROOSTING ON THE SHORE. IT'S WAITING
FOR THE WIND TO LET IT DOWN SO IT CAN
SLEEP. I OFTEN FEEL LIKE THAT SEAGULL."

Darby's mom, Patricia
(1946–2019)

Darby is a writer from
Melbourne, Australia.
(1975–?)

"DARBY, LOVE, I'M DEAD NOW. I GOT THE EMAIL
YOU SENT AFTER I DIED (EVEN THOUGH I
ONLY EVER CHECKED MY EMAIL ONCE, YEARS
AGO, IN A LIBRARY). THAT WAS AS POINTLESS
AS SENDING A SMOKE SIGNAL ON A WINDY
DAY, LOVE. BUT LET'S CALL IT A MESSAGE IN
A BOTTLE RIDING A SEA OF STARS. ANYWAY,
SOMEHOW YOU'RE WRITING WORDS FOR ME.
IT'S A BIT SILLY, LOVE. I WOULDN'T PHRASE
HALF THE THINGS HOW YOU'VE WRITTEN
THEM. AND DID I REALLY SAY SOME OF
THOSE THINGS? I PROBABLY DID. BUT YOU
CHANNELED MY SPIRIT AND CAUGHT IT. WHAT
A COLLABORATION BETWEEN THE LIVING AND
THE DEAD! YOU ARE ME AS I AM YOU. THANK
YOU, LOVE. AND REMEMBER TO STAY WARM,
EVEN THOUGH IT'S THE MIDDLE OF SUMMER."

ABOUT THE AUTHOR

Darby Hudson is a writer and poet from Melbourne, Australia. He sat and wrote under a gum tree and an old peppercorn tree by the train tracks at night after work—watching trains light up the riverbed of steel like industrial fireworks—for ten years. Now he watches life go by from the sidelines at his kitchen window. He's previously been published in *Best Australian Poems*.

Instagram: @darby_hudson
YouTube: @darby_hudson
Substack: @darbyhudson
TikTok: @darbyhudson6
Podcast: Blah Di Da (on all services)
Website: darbyhudsonart.com